Jane M. Broccolo

Like an Animal

When Being Human
Is Not Enough

ISBN: 1449554032
EAN-13: 9781449554033

*The most spiritual aspect of being human
is being an animal.*

—Instinctual Knowing

When being human is not enough...

Contents

... Enough

Quotes from Nature Sources

What vision do you hold for me, for humanity?
I hold for all of you your Majesty.

—Sweetgrass, the Dachshund

2 Like an Animal

Let their remarks roll off your back as gently
as I let your sisters roll off of mine.

—Bricabrac, the Mare

Introduction

For a long time, I was mad at the Church for putting one over on me. If God exists, how could only you and I be made in his image as the Church would have us believe? What about the rest of *Creation*?

But if God does exist, and if only we are made in his image, why wouldn't the Church also say that God is an animal since we as animals would look like him? Surely, God would not be a hollow shell, but endowed with the same set of body organs, functions, and odors that make up our own animal selves.

Priding ourselves on being human and the only ones created in the image of God, or a god, feels perverse, an ornamental headdress we wear to pretend we're a cut above the rest of the animals on the planet. We are not.

We are as vulnerable. As fierce. As dumb. As brilliant. And we are as connected to the source of our existence as any animal we attempt to reduce to a low status. Yet, we fail to bask in that connection with Source as regularly as other animals do.

I love being an animal, and the more I remember to live like one embodying the full sublimity of my animal nature, the more easily heaven's gate on earth opens for me.

Non-human animals have a strong psychic muscle to leap through that gate regardless of circumstances. In most humans that muscle is flab from lack of use.

In one extreme situation, I was forced to tap so deeply into my animal self that compassion instantly shifted my assailant's intention from murdering me, to rescuing me. I would not be alive today to write this book in praise of the animals and of being one, if it had not been for the saving grace of my animal self, my true self.

I learned to respect all animals as I would any of my human animal relatives, meaning you. All are endowed with the god- or nature given birthright to life, liberty, and the pursuit of happiness.

A right not ours to take away.

Throw the word, anthropomorphism, into the cosmic dumpster—the one with *dominion over the earth,* and *animals are our property* junk in it. People who experience animals as multidimensional, intelligent, and wise beings are often considered anthropomorphic—usually by people projecting their own human shortcomings onto them and onto the animals.

Besides having a deep rapport with various animals, I, like many of you, talk to trees. Occasionally, they talk back. You can dialog with anyone in nature as you probably are quite aware.

When quiet in nature, I ask for and receive pertinent messages from clouds, poison oak, rocks, babbling brooks, yellow jackets, hummingbirds, goats, and other animals including humans who might be around.

Maybe the messages come from the individual animate and/or *in*-animate beings themselves, or maybe they come from the omniscience permeating life and death. Or maybe I am nuts; I doubt it.

Since I am an animal and a feminine one at that, my writing is often circular, non-linear in style; no insult against feminists—I am one as well. Round like Mother Earth is all-inclusive, that's all.

The spontaneous digressions in this book occurring here and there, however erratic in sequence or content they may appear to be, are not meant to distract, but to represent the natural chaotic order of life.

Some of my statements are interpreted by a few as too direct and politically incorrect; not round at all, but too real—gritty.

It was suggested that I soften them up (dumb them down), and close the space between the lines for you. How 'awe-full' if this little book should have space for you to read into and breathe in your own true grit.

I could not fill in the blanks for you any more than I could cut out appendages of who I am, what I experience, and the intensity with which I think and feel. Self-mutilation is not my passion…anymore.

It turns out that my words are not as much a turnoff as what one literary agent professed them to be. In April, 2008, I sent her my book's first chapter, "A Born Animal", my memory of my first minute or so, of my birth.

She replied that my chapter, in her words did not "charm" her, it was a "turn-off".

Would someone who wholly embraces her/his animal self cringe from an authentically graphic description of birth?

Most, if not all, of the people I meet with health problems have issues with being an animal. I know. I was one of those people who would shudder at the sound of calling certain body parts by their names.

An anus is a good thing. Self-accepting animals don't shame it for the kind of work it does, at least not that I know of.

***

My first chapter did charm the agent after all. It became the premise for a new book she represented and sold for publication almost a year later. It's about the first five minutes of birth written by one of her longtime clients.

That book is intensely scientific, whereas, my chapter is subjective based on my own personal experience of my birth.

The agent's book is a fascinating must-read; we as human animals need to know the whys. Our animal self and other animals don't need to know why. They simply know what is, hence, they have no use for an overdeveloped intellectual frontal lobe to muddle their instinctual knowing.

A clear sense of *knowing* is the invaluable gift with which every animal human or otherwise, is endowed; whether or not we choose to tap into this precious natural resource is up to us.

When I consider the appeal of the agent's book to our insatiable intellects, a painting I often visited at the NY Metropolitan Museum comes into mind: a plump naked woman, the classic symbol of our ideal anima—the Divine Feminine embodying earth and sky—lays reclined on a lounge gazing out at her stars and the crescent moon.

Five taut scientists in black coat tails and top hats are bent over her, peering through their pince-nez, their noses barely touch her flesh.

The scientists scratch their heads, so to speak, clearly missing out on the big picture: the sacred Beauty within the universal, earthy, animal essence.

I wonder: if you were to read the agent's book she represented, of scientific research based on probing babies in utero—babies deprived by scientists of their much needed peace in the womb to prepare themselves for the world outside— would you find it weird and a turnoff that this type of search for knowledge is perfectly acceptable to us?

The author of that book insists that we could

never know what our own first five minutes of birth are like. That's what he *thinks*.

His oversight brings to mind parents who abuse their babies with the excuse that a baby could not remember.

Every animal remembers.

***

If anything in this book is uncomfortable for you, please see it as an invitation to go within and explore perhaps a fear, or a denial of some exquisite quality hidden deep inside yourself beneath any shockwave you might feel pulsing through you.

Also, as minor as this may seem: this book is endowed on purpose with grammatical errors regarding pronouns, i.e., the cow *who*, instead of, the cow *that*—our palatable way of reducing other animals to mere things to avoid recognizing the live, feeling, and aware beings they are.

***

I talk a lot about a sixteen-year-old—one-hundred-twelve in dog years—mini-dachshund, Sweetgrass.

She is small, but she is mighty.

Small, but mighty. That is how I hope you will come to view this book of personal contents— dis-jointed bones stripped bare of the lies they once supported, piled together to make a loose skeletal representation of the animal I have become: part ground-up coarse to scratch at the most brittle corner of the human heart; the other part ground extra fine to hopefully slip gently in.

~

Remembering…

*I am the tears of joy our mother the earth gave up
so I may fall back on her.*

—The Rain

1

A Born Animal

Like any ordinary, unnatural, and uncomplicated birth, mine was no more fun for me at the time than it was for my mother. But in hindsight, the doctor and nurses were kind and caring people, and my birth—thanks to a recent viewpoint from a dog—now feels like an adventure to me, so much so that I am glad caesarian births were not the norm then.

I was almost forty before I would breathe my way back to remembering in the safety of a Sandra Ray rebirthing workshop, what took place in that loud lit room in Glen Cove, New York, under the fluorescent light at the end of my mother's tunnel.

The moment immediately after the robotic steel hands squeezed my head and yanked me out into the cold light, four of the Five Senses plus an emotional sense were there with me, ready to inform me that whether I liked it or not, this is life, baby.

First, Sight appeared: though our eyes are shut when we come into the world face down, I definitely remember noticing the pulsating anus through the other side of my wafer thin eyelids. I attribute this particular introduction as my first role model, obvious in the fact that later, people would sometimes refer to me by its nickname.

Next, I would have to say that since I cannot to this day recall feeling the still visible impact of the forceps on my skull, Touch first announced itself to me through the slap on my rump. Ouch.

Needless to say, Sound kicked in immediately. No doubt about it, I was hearing my outrage at being touched.

Rage completely overwhelmed me when the strangers with masked mouths were laughing at, or was it—with—my indignant cries as the balding gray guy wearing glasses cut off my umbilical cord—my only way back—too soon before I was ready to face my new world.

My way back trashed, panic took over. As I was held dangling over my poor mother's limp and unconscious body, yearning to fall back on it, my first impression of my mother's face came from the anguish shaping it. Without my mother's eyes or arms open to welcome me, my heart sank with a sense of grief, isolation, and shame.

I am sorry was my first unspeakable regret when I a minute or so, old.

Finally, the sense of Smell: what a stinky animal I am, the collapsed lining of my mother's womb sticking to me; comforting before, but I can see in the strangers' faces, it is too earthy to endure, let alone taste.

I haven't a clue as to when Taste came to me.

What I will not forget is that the dark, murky realm from where we all come infused me with the salt of the earth—the essence of being an animal encoded in every cell of my body.

~

I wish you had arms to wrap around me now.
I have many arms around you. If you feel
real hard, you will know their caress.

—Granite Rock

2

Coming of Age at Four
(in Human Years)

My impish toddler hands carefully tucked seeds into the warm sand bed.

I then sprinkled water from my father's old tin can, wetting my dreams of juicy cantaloupes in summer.

Later, my dreams awoke. Green, tender arms emerged from sheets of sand and stretched across their grainy bed. I imagined their arms' length long enough to reach and wrap around the August sun. They in turn, felt my touch.

Like an animal, I was complete in my connection to Earth, to Sun, to the warm grains of sand slipping through my fingers.

"Pull them out, now!" the woman ordered my stunned father who had no idea how the cantaloupes got there.

Without hesitation, or intended harm, my father ripped my cantaloupe dreams out by the roots, leaving a hole in my tiny heart; a glorious hole that would soon have me falling through groundbreaking adventures into my earthy, animal nature as I turned away from a normal life.

Much to my delight, I am still falling.

~

*We cannot create the damnation of 'lesser'
creatures who are eternally deemed angels.*

—Little White Goat

3

Invoking My Animal Essence

It was only natural, aside from the cantaloupe event, that at an early age I would begin to feel more at home with non-human animals than with human ones.

Humans did not act like what we were made out to be.

How could I feel safe with them again after seeing my dear feathered friends have their heads chopped off right below our kitchen window? My mother and I had rescued their sweet bodies months before when they were mere chicks soaked in the cold rain; lumps of wet, matted fuzz with beaks crying for help.

Witnessing the slaughter of my hen buddies made me sensitive to the abuse rendered toward my other animal friends.

Once, I was strapped to the seat of a goat cart tethered to my goat pal running scared. It was the first time I was aware of what it is to feel humiliated. But it was not my own shame that I was feeling in my body. It was the goats. The goat's despair gave me the experience of how it feels to be victimized by the consciousness of an eighteen year-old boy treating himself to a laugh at our expense. I felt it in my body as surely as the goat felt it in his. It was a feeling of contraction, a folding in on us—a hunching over internally.

I also started realizing I could communicate my feelings and thoughts to Bricabrac the bay horse where I lived better than to my human counterparts. The mare would gently roll my older sisters off her back whenever I whispered into her ear that they had acted mean to me. I liked her special way of showing me we were best friends.

By age five, I conquered my dread of spiders by saving their lives. Many daddy-long-legs in our house stopped short in their tracks at my unspoken command. They made it easy for me to coax them into jars, and toss them back to nature before my father—under the orders of my terrified sisters—could crush them.

Decades later, with a cold slice of ham in hand, I had the sudden chill of realization that the texture of dead pig flesh felt the same as the flesh of a human cadaver. I immediately declared myself a practicing non-cannibal.

My meatless diet soon afterwards saved me from surgery due to the subsequent disappearance from my body of thyroid disease. I later learned that meat and dairy products are far from healthy for the human body. They can do more harm to us than throw a thyroid off balance. I didn't know back then that eating animal parts was a major cause of heart disease, diabetes, and cancer.

My new sense of well-being—a welcomed side-effect of a meatless diet—inspired me to learn meditation under the guidance of a teacher from India. He was a Jain of the Hindu sect that strives for non-violence toward all living beings.

One evening while meditating alone, I suddenly found myself *floating* on the ceiling, looking down at an animal. It seemed small and defenseless in the empty space engulfing it.

My heart instantly *reached out* to the vulnerable creature below, prompting me to leave at the speed

of light my heightened awareness to help and pro-
tect this animal, my body.

Soon after that eye-opening experience of actually *seeing* myself as an animal, I began witnessing that people performing on stage or having a
heart-to-heart talk with me, would dissolve(sort of
like the animal on the cover of this book)into
light and return a split second later in full form.

Your pet has the same experience. When s/he
seems to be looking through you, s/he is; seeing
only your light.

In an article for lay people about *String Theory*,
I read that all visible matter is in reality, energy
encoded with information. More lay articles I read
were on *Quantum Physics* and Einstein's *Unified
Field Theory* describing our multidimensional universe and the invisible connectedness within, and
between everything.

We, as animals, have an innate ability to see
the illusion of form dissolve into its true energy
state of what many would describe as love.

We can have the visual as well as kinesthetic
experience of the poetic all one or universal love,
the Beauty embodying and connecting all existence—highlighted in Buddhism and other enlight-
ening belief systems.

Having been brought up under the iron rule of

the Church, I was surprised to learn that anima is Latin for 'soul'. In the traditional language of the Church, animals are attributed to having souls.

Isn't it romantic to think that a cockroach has a soul? And that s/he is connected to us by a unifying energy of encoded information, a universal love?

Many times during my years on Madison Avenue as a copywriter, I could not stop myself from talking to clients at lunch about the sacred beauty of a cockroach. I could not shut my mouth about the arrogance of humanity to regard ourselves as a superior species based on egocentric human definitions of what intelligence is.

Our name, Homo Sapiens, translates as wise and intelligent, yet, we may not have the know-how or flexibility to make it past our 250,000 more or less years of Homo Sapiens existence.

The cockroach has brilliantly thrived for the past three-hundred-million years. It was already here seventy million years before the dinosaurs.

It's immortal compared to us.

Feeling hopelessly deprived in the ad business, I went to school after hours to learn about our mind-body-spirit connection and the healing affects of acupressure, energy therapy, intuition, spirit medium-ship, telepathy, hypnosis, and a few alternative methods the American Medical Association is lobbying to incorporate for themselves.

After certification, I weaned myself off of Mad Ave and began my practice as an energy therapist for human and on occasion, non-human animals, and later as a medium—a telepathic go-between for humans and the deceased.

During a session, the encoded energies—or souls—of my client's three deceased dogs unexpectedly came into the room. Their *presence* was apparent to my client as well. The detailed verbal information that channeled through me from his dogs was confirmed correct by him.

For a long time I kept this particular talent under wraps. Following my heart's desire to serve as a pet medium to help close the communication gap between human and non-human animals was not an option I would have given myself back then for fear of ridicule.

That was then.

My passion for animals combined with excruciating pain in witnessing the treatment of them in our country and all over the world pushed me to take action. I had to completely come out of the closet to serve animals.

And so I did. I founded TalksWithPets as a means to open up dialogues between people and their pets for the purpose of deepening understanding between them. It was a small step, but a good starting point for people to experience the depth of their animals' inner being as something beyond cute looks.

As clients responded to the unique intelligence and wisdom of their pets, some eventually developed a concern for all animals tame and wild.

Some did not.

I soon learned that understanding through the intellect is not the best route to compassion.

TalksWithPets evolved into AnimalSelfEpowerment linking us to the subliminal place within our own animal selves. The silent, non-thinking, universal state of mind is where we commune with animals and all of nature on an equal and inspiring level.

When we venture deep beneath the surface of our minds into our animal essence of knowing that we are all connected beyond the superficial separation of species, we have the breadth of compassion to embrace all life.

We are waking up as the truth behind the self-serving illusions we have created for ourselves—for the purpose of exploiting other animals, nature, and the planet—can no longer be denied.

It is not okay anymore to live like the cute spoiled

brats we've been, unrelated to the rest of creation and, or, evolution.

***

Abe Lincoln said we cannot be wholly human until we have mercy for all creatures.

I add that we cannot have mercy for all creatures until we first whole bodily accept one bare, beautiful fact:

We are essentially animals having a human experience.

We need only remember.

~

Never doubt your wings.

—Bald Eagle

4

The Essentials of Being
an Animal

When we evolve into the animals we are, we have instant access to the essential abilities of any animal. The ability to be:

In a conscious state of real knowing; instead of limited by short-sighted human logic.

Engaged in absolute integrity; instead of caged in a false and unnatural morality.

Clear; instead of confused.

Whole, together in harmony; instead of fractured in isolation.

Empathic and telepathic.

Alive and present in the moment—able to face any situation with emergent resourcefulness and courage.

Able to leap from fear to love in a heartbeat.

~

You, too, can learn when not to sting.

—Buzz from Yellow Jacket

5

My Father
Was a Complete Animal

He was not the stereotype one attributes to humans who vent their libido and rage all over the place. My father was of a different breed.

I never saw him as violent, physically or verbally. Not once did he lose his temper or growl at me or my sisters, or use unsavory language in our presence.

He was a gentle man in the archaic sense. He put others' needs—his family's, his friends, his enemies—before his own.

My father put everyone before him to the point my mother would wake up screaming in the night whenever the firehouse alarm sounded a mile away, and my father—the good volunteer fireman that he was until weeks before his death—would leap from his warm bed in winter to save a house.

My mother said my father's selfless, kind-hearted manner was thick-skulled; nothing ever seemed to faze him.

His lab mix canine friend, Annie, was like him. His twin soul if such a thing exists.

Like my father, nothing about anyone ever bothered Annie. She was kind to everyone, human or otherwise. She was the most gentle, most patient, most annoying being—besides my father—I have ever met.

In fact, she was such a people pleasing yes-dog I wanted to kill her at times.

I was mean. Once when I felt helpless from having tried to ease her arthritic pain, I told her to shut up after hearing her constant moans from the other room.

She never moaned again. My father asked me if I had hit Annie, said she had changed since my last visit. I told him, no, and that was the truth.

But I had gotten through to her.

***

Now that my father and Annie are long gone, I have a different, more true-to-life picture of them.

I realize that my father and Annie, in their pure simplicity, let everyone in—*every*one got to them—to the point they *had* to be big-hearted.

They had to stretch with unwavering grace in embracing everyone regardless of the passing insult inflicted upon them. It was the only way they could live out their long, vibrant, and joyful lives to the fullest.

Which is what they did.

They turned the other cheek, so to speak, but not in a way that diminished their inner dignity. They were over-the-top generous in their acceptance of human foibles.

If they had not been magnanimous, they would have needed to establish boundaries and be like a lot of people; fractured and suspicious, who like me, often let only a select few in, rationing out kindness when convenient or tax deductible.

My father and Annie were complete animals in their embodiment of the trait we esteem the most, but exhibit the least.

***

Compassion is inborn in all animals, at least all mammals. The true story about the elephant who stopped by the side of the road to lift a jeep off a wounded driver is one example. There are many incidents we've been made aware of regarding compassion as an animal trait.

Marc Bekoff's book, *Minding Animals: Awareness, Emotions, and Heart*, is chock-full of compassionate animal stories.

***

Imagine being big-hearted as the complete animals we potentially are.

Never stuck in an unforgiving net of thick-skulled morality.

Never living small behind borders.

Never afraid to fully enjoy who we are.

~

We are the pillars of your strength.
The journey of your life.
Your destiny standing still for you to catch up
and dig your roots into our soul.

—Redwood Tree

6

Finding God in a Strip Joint

They say our present reality is a quick read of our entire past. It seems moments ago, I was a prissy New York copywriter running past strip joints in Time Square to some high-end ad agency meeting.

I felt smug rushing past those places, thinking how smart I was in my pinstriped suit, a demure hint of promise peeping through the long slit in my skirt, the soft sound of my high-heeled pumps clicking on the smooth sidewalk. I was at the top of my game, or so I believed.

***

This late afternoon, my legs chill in black fishnet on my drive up the switchbacks to Flagstaff in my little silver Mazda, a new dent in the left fender.

Shivering with just enough body heat to keep the metal on my crimson lace garter belt from turning cold, I think about the turns I've taken through time incarnate to find myself presently at the door of those distant dark places; doors perhaps no longer existing in Times Square, but still yielding their threshold at the dive where I'm headed.

Traces of gold from the sun gradually retreat from the tall fir and pine weighted down from last night's snowfall.

I pretend that the trees are my receiving line on the sidelines of the dirty white carpet of snow laid out before me.

The curvy motion of my car combined with the stale air inside, makes me stomach-sick. Do I have the guts to go through with this?

This morning, a client asked me to invoke the spirit of Mother Mary to help her forgive herself for success on Wall Street. Tonight, I expose myself to a different kind of icon, the carnal kind without mercy.

Living at opposite ends of the human spectrum is a challenge I give myself to stretch to Rilke-esque extremes where I learn in the empty space between.

Stripping my soul at Happy Hour is a refreshing way for me to strip away the last residue of Catholic shame for having been born like an animal, and of female flesh.

***

My Mazda climbs to 8,000 feet as I look beyond the cliff's edge at the bleak abyss below. I remember the times I hurled myself out of a plane at thirty-five hundred feet to rise above my dread of heights. My legs would tremble and give out from under me on a third-floor fire escape.

I continue the climb, confident in the quiet stillness of the falling snow.

As I snake up and around the mountain's edge, I wonder if it was a mistake to have dropped the status, false security, and money the ad business gave me. Has it been worth it to put my mind to rest to expose my soul, instead?

My therapy work at resorts does fulfill my need to help people feel better, my penance for the empty promises my ads drove home to them every day in the media.

***

I park a block from my gig in hopes no one will
see me wolf down a pint of cold pasta.

What'll I do? I never danced publicly any-
where before, with or without clothing. Never. I
was too shy, too self-conscious—too scared that
my body would put on an embarrassing display if
it ever got into the rhythm.

I take a swig of water from my bottle, swish
away traces of spinach between my teeth and
swallow. I pat my lips dry. I color them red.

Showtime. With both feet on the ground, I
hoist myself out of the safe confinement of my
little car. I shudder from the cold, and shut and
lock the door quickly to wrap my long gray tweed
coat, a Salvation Army Store special, around my
legs. My spiked black vinyl heels are out of place
on the iced cobbled-stone street leading to my
stage door.

I take a deep breath and push against the
door's heavy metal. I cross the threshold and step
into a haze of smoke and blue shirts. Not the blue
shirts that white-collared men in suits might
wear—but the ones with coarse sleeves rolled up
over brown arms with elbows on the tables and
calloused hands clutching beer glasses full of
the promise of immediate salvation.

I hurry past the blue shirts, the beer glasses,

and waver up three wobbly stairs leading onto the creaky wood stage.

On stage, I break into a cocky strut and begin my long journey across the square pedestal built by relatives of these drunken men. I stop in the middle. My body is dead weight as I turn and face my bleary-eyed audience.

Loud jeers ensue. I slip off my coat. A few men straddle their chairs and lean forward against the backs like animals in pounce stance. My black satin blouse and matching buttoned up floor length skirt are a thin veneer between the men and me.

I dare to act a predator pacing above them. My coat, dangling from my hand, tails behind me as I swoosh back past the rows of blue shirts and beer glasses. This time I look directly into eyes, every detail made vivid by the intensity between us. I take note of red framing the dark spheres, eyes drowning in the blood of their tears.

I am oddly at home with these animals.

I turn again and continue back across the stage toward the boom box the bouncer set up. Once there, I stop, bend my knees, and keep my back straight and legs together. Like a robotic lady, I reach to turn on the tape.

"Can-Can" blares out. The corny, thumping

rhythm helps me grind my hips, a warm-up for the twenty minutes onstage.

The animals clap, whistle, hiss, and howl watching me act like an animal as well. But unlike them, I have no shackles keeping me from stealing freely through alien territory in blind search of the unknown.

They like me. Good. I breathe deeper down into my body to accept myself more. I cannot. I'm an idiot to be here.

I freeze.

Having nowhere to hide, I escape further into my audience's eyes for protection. As a last resort, my heart *reaches out* to them with love. I feel a connection. The dance begins.

My body takes lead over my mind, this time an animal confident in its earthy element. Moving with the roar of music and applause, I am surprised to feel peace and stillness inside me.

No longer glazed, the men's eyes clearly show me tenderness—the kind a lioness displays when licking her cubs clean. Encouraged, I dance in their glow, forgetting I cannot dance.

The music flows through my veins like good wine, the blood of Christ. Slowly, I undo the buttons holding my skirt together.

The last button undone at my waist, my skirt

slips to the floor, lifting a final veil from the men's eyes to reveal their own nakedness to me.

Falling into sudden Beauty in these eyes, I step down off my pedestal and glide around and around the men, dancing in awe as I would with a newborn baby.

***

The twenty minutes gone by, the boom box off, the men raise themselves off their seats in silence, and stand in line side by side, as if having received a holy communion.

If that is not puzzling enough, each man then gently shakes my hand in gratitude as I walk past him on my way out the door.

Like an animal, God had come baring our souls.

Knowing…

All animals, including humans, yearn to experience Beauty—the only real and safe place in the world.

Beauty is the act of savoring the absolute truth that all is well.

It is the journey one suffers to ultimately come around to it.

Sometimes Beauty is disguised in hate as Love shouting to get our attention.

Sometimes it is shrouded in blood and gore as Death wanting to take us home.

Sometimes it is hidden in the Unknown for us to unearth its vast terrain.

Wherever we are, Beauty is there for us to lift the veil from our hearts so we may know it.

It is there to fall back on, always around for us to lapse into.

Someone who has nothing to lose by violently going beyond the pale of human decency could be closer to Beauty than we who keep our horror under tight rein with silky pretenses.

In his raw and unbridled brute honesty, a certain rapist once had no human restraints to keep him from making a fast leap from fear and hate to where Beauty waits.

—A Field of Cows

7

It Takes a Beast to Know Beauty

It's two a.m. I'm speeding through Wyoming in a rental car. Windows are rolled up tight. Static is on the radio. Gas gauge is flashing empty. A black void hangs over me in my rearview mirror. If I chase my headlights, I can keep the void from catching up to me. I cannot face being lost.

I look for a sign, any sign to tell me I'm not alone in the middle of nowhere.

Finally, one looms out at me from the shoulder: Cheyenne.

Cheyenne? This is not the way back to my hotel in Denver. I've been driving for at least an hour in the opposite direction.

On empty, the car sputters to a crawl. How can this be happening to me? Me, who gave up sex so I could be safe and protected by a god I don't believe in.

I steer the car over the shoulder. It occurs to me no car has been in sight for the last hour. The night swirls in around me, chilling me in fear. A gutsy New Yorker who rides the subway at three a.m., yet I'm a wimp in the dark since my uncle yelled "boo" at me when I was two, sitting alone in the dark in my high chair.

I shut off the radio and listen. My heart pounds hard against ribs that feel like prison bars. A thought of the man with the hooked arm who sneaks up on parked cars in campfire stories enters my mind and takes over. I breathe deep and try to mediate to calm down, but fear has other plans for me.

Slouched in the driver's seat, my arms clasped tight across my chest, I force my shut eyes open enough to see what's out there.

Shadows are sliding over the ground. Just bushes, I tell myself.

Bushes don't slide over the ground.

I can't take being scared of nothing. Please God, *anything* but nothing.

Suddenly light begins flooding my car. I turn

my head around to look out the rear window. Two headlights in the distance are quickly coming my way. Thank God, I am saved.

I bolt out of my car. Wind lashes hair across my eyes, my cotton skirt against my thighs. I fling myself in front of the headlights of the oncoming truck. It slows down and stops. I run up and in my excitement, bump my belly up against the left headlight. My hand brushes over the gritty surface of the fender as I rush over to the passenger window and peer in. A blond man is at the wheel; a dark-haired man, his passenger.

"Hi. I was so scared you wouldn't stop. I'm out of gas. Is there a gas station somewhere you could drive me to?" I'm panting out of breath.

They sit there staring out at me.

"Please, you can't just leave me out here alone." God, they're dense. "Please, it's dangerous out here." Still panting.

They look at one another. Big decision. Finally, the dark one pushes his door wide open, and steps down and out of the truck to let me in.

"Thank you. For a minute I thought you were just going to leave me here."

They don't talk to me, yet I feel safe climbing into this pick-up truck. It's powder blue, the same colored truck the bread man used to drive when I was a kid. I miss the smell of his sweaty cigar and bread still hot from the oven as I sit between these two brooding men.

Their crude silence begins to comfort me.

As we drive off leaving my rental car behind, I glance back over my shoulder and feel sad for it. Poor little abandoned thing. I hope it'll be okay.

I gaze blankly at the road ahead taking me farther into night. A hand crawls on my thigh. Great, they think I'm a pickup.

"Look, I just want you to take me to a phone." I turn to the dark man on my right, and grab his thick hand.

The hand is not moved.

"Take your paw off me or stop the truck, let me out, and I'll walk."

They stop the truck. The dark one opens his door, gets out, and lets me out. I get out. The door slams shut behind me. A hand slams down on my mouth. I do not get to walk. I shrivel like a little ball orbiting the palm of this coarse hand of fate. It reeks of hamburger grease.

"You resist and you're dead before it's over," says the owner of the greasy hand.

This is what I get for forcing myself to be celibate for nine months: my trapped animal energy had churned into extreme frustration, a kind of violence that attracts the violence of this different breed of caged-in animal.

My only way out is in, deep inside myself. Like an animal in its true power, I've got to be present in this moment if I want to make it to the next alive.

Fear, rage, the *shoulds*, *what ifs*—the human mind clutter—I drop it by the side of the road. Death is my only alternative in this moment.

The moment in its sordidness begins to feel fresh; clean as crisp, washed sheets hanging on the line to dry. A sharp, high-frequency intensity begins surging through every fiber of my being. I am immediately alert and in control like an animal.

The two men spread a blanket on the ground as if we're having a picnic. The dark one knocks me down and grabs my blouse—my new white cotton blouse.

"Please don't tear it!"

He goes to unbutton it, instead.

"Are your hands clean?" I sit up straight. I'm aware of my hand delicately brushing the blanket clean of imaginary crumbs.

He stares at his hands in the dark.

"You do it then."

I begin undoing my blouse. My thumb connects me to the hard, smooth circle of what's left of my civilized world—the button.

"This is a sin," I say, having no idea where anything I say to them is coming from. My animal instincts are talking for me.

"What?"

"You remind me of my brother." I don't have a brother.

He backs off.

Incest is more perverse to him than rape and murder. Or maybe something deep inside him does not want to hurt me.

The blond—still on his knees—quietly waits.

I'm at a loss for words facing two men on their knees.

My feet slip off my shoes. In the distance, I see why. I jump to my feet and start running toward the highway. A huge truck is rushing to my rescue as the two men bolt up and run back to their own truck.

I scurry like a mouse into the middle of the road with my skinny arms flailing at the monster truck coming toward me.

Sucked in by the force of it, I hurl myself out of the way of this *savior* just in time as I feel its fury speed past me with intent to kill, if that's what I want.

Winded, I scamper across the asphalt toward

the black emptiness on the other side of the road, my bare feet slapping the pavement in perfect rhythm with the rapist from the powder blue truck coming up fast behind me.

Gasping for breath, the memory of how I used to outrun the guys in track back in school enters my mind giving me hope for escape.

The rapist tackles me to the ground.

Crushed under his weight, there's no time to indulge in feeling like a victim. I opt fast to feel grounded, not pinned down. Flat on my back, I surrender like a submissive dog strong enough to give in, to be vulnerable to a noble power within.

The earth supports me in my choice. It feels warm and soft as though breathing beneath me, through me, rocking me in its sweet breath. I want it to pull me under.

The rapist, in missionary position ejaculates in seconds through the sound of a whimper. Raped by him is more innocuous than making love.

The question, what is our mission together, floats through my empty mind.

He keeps moving inside me, a repetitive dripping faucet kind of torture.

"Did you come, yet?" I know darn well he did.

"Yes."

"Oh...then...what are you doing?"

"I want you to come."

I pant like a toy poodle, faking an orgasm with care not to upstage his previous whimper.

"Oh, that was wonderful. Thank you," I coo.

***

Frozen in the silence beneath his body, I know he's going to kill me. He must, the stars are lighting my face as brightly as they are his.

Those stars: Heavenly eyes twinkling down at me over Cheyenne's outback. I cry out to them in silence through my whole body, insisting they recognize their fire in me.

I don't want to die. The earth feels soft under me. I had never noticed before the stars in color.

And those shadows still whispering over the ground—my demons moments ago—now my angels perhaps concerned about my welfare. I cannot die without knowing who they are.

Without warning, I see a child's face in the face of this rapist. A tiny face with blood streaking over it like a river flooded and forced off course; a face of a child whose only experience of love came from the backhand of people's bitterness.

Is this face the rapist's face as a child? Or is it my life passing before me?

I think of the rapist's sad, sickly whimper in announcing his coming, his awkward innocence in wanting me to come.

This man's contempt for me is a way, as shoddy as it is, to make contact with another being. The only way he can grasp how to save himself from being ignored, invalidated, nonexistent—dead.

Face to face with my own pain reflected in him, the rapist suddenly looks familiar to me. The rapist *is* me.

He clenches his hand on a rock by my head.

"You're beautiful," I blurt out, stunned by what I am hearing, knowing it is true.

I sense his hand soften on the rock.

"Yes, you are. You *are* beautiful. You are *beautiful.*"

We are both transfixed by the sudden passing through of Beauty melting us in its wake.

***

"Come on, I'll take you to a phone," he mumbles getting up and fumbling with his zipper.

I draw in the Wyoming night deep to the bottom of my lungs. I feel giddy.

"No, I'll stay here."

He stands still, his body strong, staring out into the distance.

"I can't leave you out here alone. It's dangerous," he says, keeping his eye on nothing.

I have to stay. How long can he keep separate from his violence—the very thing he now senses as dangerous out there?

He walks away. I jump up and run, hop, skip after him, twirling by his side, like a girl scout in my green skirt. I'm absurd. I don't care. I am *alive*.

"I'll walk you to your truck. I want to say goodbye to your friend."

We cross the highway and walk up to his truck. I glide over to the passenger leaning against it.

"Bye, thank you!" I bellow out to the passenger.

The passenger looks stupefied as if I'm crazy and he's guilty.

***

I watch the two men drive away in the powder blue truck. I then turn and run through the fields, my bare feet sucking in the soft, moist, grassy earth.

I see cows. Cows, everywhere.

"So, you were my shadows in the night, you

wonderful creatures, you." I run around and around, circling every random cow. Their necks curve in my wake. Their heads tilt toward me, perhaps to get a better look.

I thank every blade of grass until the sparkling sky fades into gray.

From the horizon, a procession of pale head-lights—like eyes sick with bile—crawls through the dull mist. It's Monday morning.

***

It seems like hours that I'm standing by the side of the road trying to wave down a car. My arms tire. July's temperature rises. I feel grungy, help-less, and exposed. So this is the morning after.

In the exhaustion that sweeps over me, I *slip back* to when I was three, standing ankle deep in the dust of a circus, left by my family who thought I was with them.

As I sink deeper into feeling lost and un-wanted, my rapist's words come cantering on a pony kicking up that trail of dust in my mind.

"I can't leave you out here alone. It's dangerous." Not *really*.

Peace comes over me whenever I think about that night a long time ago. How alive and present I was, second nature to an animal.

There were no lies to lay heavily on my heart, snuffing out the moment of truth. No smoke-screens to blur my vision. No pretense to sedate the ever present intensity of life.

The rapist's contempt for me was more honest than any man's love for me had been. His transparency triggered in me the clarity of an animal to see what I needed to do to save my life.

We were strangers, yet I *knew* his scent like it was my own. I knew it well enough to track the stench of fear over a thousand miles to meet him on common ground—and fall with him into our clear state of absolution.

***

Usually when I told this story, people tried to shame me for having had no skin under my nails to show for my courage that night.

They criticized me for not feeling angry, for feeling good, for not acting out their idea of a liberated woman, a divine feminine.

I told them in all honesty that the rapist did me no harm.

The morally indignant obsessed with their opinion that I am in denial, refused to hear me.

"How can you forgive that animal? How can you not have the decency to feel rage after having been raped?"

I met Beauty. That's how.

~

I was imprisoned in a futuristic world.
   It was against the law to feel.
   *We were numbed down with nano-detectors
pinned to our bodies, monitoring every inch of our
skin for the possibility of sin.*

   —A flash-back, or -forward, from the beach

8

Empathy, an Animal Thing

This is the third time tonight I have to leave the trailer bunk.

Her dreams interrupted, my dachshund sighs under the comforter.

"I'll be right back, Sweetgrass." As if she didn't know the routine. I put on my jacket, open the tin pan door, and descend into wet October blackness.

Relentless cold rain falls hard on my bare head. I squat on soggy ground. My head rotates on its axis as my ears and eyes focus on the possibility of encountering a grizzly bear, mountain lion, or pack of wolves—all who might have gotten wind that I often come out here at night.

Cringing from the cold, I remember the animal instinct to breathe deep as though my body were stretching a hand out to bargain with it. My breathy acceptance of the cold warms my body and maybe, the temperature outside.

I remember to absorb the Silence between the drops of rain. The sensation of the rain falling, making a splash on my head, begins to feel like cool wet kisses from nowhere.

Ignored again, no one desiring my flesh and bones, I scurry back into the trailer. I have to admit, underneath my complaining I do get a thrill out of living like an animal. Present and ready for anything. An exhilarating high, a reason as good as any to live, it is.

I lunge back under the comforter. Sweetgrass snores on the other side of the bed. In two hours the fawn will be coming out of the woods for his bottle, not caring how exhausted I might be from my nocturnal communes with nature.

***

Seven a.m. Like clockwork the wild fawn appears, as predictable as the still heavy rain. Sweetgrass tenses on the bed annoyed that the fawn is back.

I tell her I'll be only a moment as I slide off

the bed to face the wet outdoors again.

With the cold rain slapping me in the face, I run through it across the open field to the well. I remember to stand back before opening the spigot. A lot of good that does me. The faucet squirts me with splintered ice before gushing water at me. After a few brisk strokes across my teeth with my frozen toothbrush, I fill a glass with water to mix with the fawn's breakfast formula.

Sweetgrass barks at me from the trailer, angry that the 'wild child' always gets fed first. The fawn is nonchalant. He knows I'll feed him. From across the drenched field, he darts a sharp glance into my eyes, piercing me down through my body.

He turns and prances toward the yurt. With total assuredness, he waits for me to rush over and heat his formula on the stove inside. I love being his slave.

***

The fawn is how I got to spend a month here in one of the last wild places in America—the extreme northwestern corner of Montana.

The people with the deed to the land I'm on left him in my care for a month. They found him when he was a day old. Hearing the fawn's cries as he stood bawling over his dead mother's gunned-down body was more than their hearts could bear. They immediately scooped him up into their arms and stole him home with them. They knew it was illegal to rescue wildlife. There was a season for killing deer, but saving them had no season. It was against the law, period.

***

I stand by the stove, peeking through the yurt window at him. He's still covered with white spots as if his maker had spilled Clorox on his fur. He looks diaphanous but under his coat, he is the real thing.

The baby formula tests warm on my wrist. I inhale the old familiar scent of fake mother's milk as I open the door to find the fawn's nose nuzzled up against it. I step outside and lean up against him with the bottle.

Sweetgrass yelps again from the bunk in the trailer at the other end of the field. She knows that when the fawn is done with breakfast, I will hand the bottle over to her to lick it clean to the last drop.

Shivering in the cold rain, lulled by the sound of the fawn suckling, his nose as wet and smooth as the bottle's latex nipple, his nostrils expanding and contracting—I would like a latex copy of those nostrils—I slip into reverie, drinking in the little things that I love about this place:

The sweet smell of sawdust mixed with grass for the compost toilet in the outhouse too far away from the trailer. The humid scent in the garden of dying green tomatoes. The cranky, spattering well. And my body chilled with my wondering if my naked toes will get frostbitten as the fawn takes his time warming his insides.

I see my relationship with the fawn as two animals made vulnerable by fear and community rejection, left alone to survive Me in my somewhat imagined danger—he, in real danger as he was two nights ago.

***

I had woken up in total terror. Not a panic attack where my chest feels as though it's caving in, crushing me to death, but a feeling far more extreme.

My lips were curled up above my gum line the way I saw Sweetgrass's lips curl once in Arizona when wild boar were chasing her.

My stomach, lungs, intestines—all of my organs felt scrunched up, convulsing in fear. I could not move on the bed. The feeling, emotional and physical, was so shocking to my system, I remember thinking this is what a deer feels when hunted.

Then it dawned on me that the fawn was in trouble; I was feeling *his* fear.

The next morning, he showed up with gashes on his side and hip.

***

The fawn and I had deeply bonded during those weeks I was there. An energetic link had formed, sending impulses between us; neurons traveling through invisible pathways, homing into our separate bodies, communicating through a language of feelings and sensations.

Empathy is a full-bodied sensation, and one of our greatest information systems for accessing what could be life-saving data, as is telepathy; two precious communication skills between animals that most people keep stuffed away inside themselves, never to be appreciated by them or by the rest of us.

Imagine how truly empathetic we'd be if we actually used these two gifts of our animal nature.

You are the most intelligent one in the world
as far as I can see.
    But I am the only one you <u>can</u> see.
Precisely.

—Grey Dove

9

No Human Left Behind

A red hot light bulb explodes in Sweetgrass' stomach, a vision in my dream that jolts me out of sleep. Sweetgrass, her face bent over mine, is staring at me in the dark, moaning.

I suddenly realize that I forgot to put the takeout container of spicy-hot chili in the fridge when I came home earlier that night. I had left it on the floor when I crouched down to pet her.

I jump out of bed to see if she has gotten into it. She has, and her water bowl is bone dry.

***

The vision in my dream was a telepathic call for help from Sweetgrass for me to stop the burning in her belly.

Another night, two big dogs approach me in a dream. I wake up, not because I'm scared, but because Sweetgrass is lying close to me, growling loud into my ear while she still sleeps. Most likely, she is dreaming about protecting me from the two dogs in my own dream.

Another telepathic event happened between Sweetgrass and me following our first visit to an inn in Sedona, Arizona.

While I sat in the welcome office, Sweetgrass was out exploring the inn grounds. That night while we were asleep, I saw her running in my dream through the foliage around the inn, and right before my eyes, she shape-shifted into a peacock.

The next day, the owner of the inn told me they once had two peacocks in their care on the property.

I assume that Sweetgrass tapped into peacock residual energy lingering there and telepathically transmitted a picture of the evidence into my dream.

***

Telepathy occurs as a transmittance of insights in the form of thoughts or images from the mind of one animal to the mind of another, whereas, empathy transmits insights in the form of emotions and physical feelings from the body of one animal to the body of another; this is how I experience these two aspects of *animal communication.*

Telepathy is often referred to as, mental telepathy, a form of communication between minds. And so, empathy ought to be called according to my book, *physica*l telepathy, since it's a transmittance of information between bodies.

Mental and physical telepathies are traits found to exist in plants as well as in animals. The book, *The Secret Life of Plants,* by Peter Tomkins and Christopher Bird, talks about the sensitivity of plants to their human emotional and mental environments.

We need to catch up to our *earthy* relatives when it comes to using our animal skills.

Their internet makes ours look under-developed, primitive. And their intelligence is smart enough to know that no one species is more intelligent than the other. Different, that's all. We know this is true though most of us wouldn't dare think it.

Hopefully, no human left behind; only our illusions of grandeur.

Insatiable guilt keeps you (humanity) from moving beyond your condemnation of non-human animals as inferior creatures.

Guilt feeds your ego while keeping you from facing the beast in your own mirror.

—Babbling Brook

10

Dumb Animal

I cannot forget this caption under an elk photo: "An elk catching some rays...apparently oblivious to the remains of his wolf-killed brethren being finished off by coyotes a few hundred yards away."

Oblivious? Not by a long shot. It looked to me like the elk had his eye on the human animal behind the zoom lens in the distance. Or maybe the elk, in his innate animal wisdom, was simply relaxing in the acceptance of nature taking its course.

Or maybe—the elk is a dumb animal as the caption implies. Who knows? The 'ors' are endless.

Who knows what is behind millions of us having dinner, feeling at home with violence roaring on the TV, not a few hundred, but a few yards away from where we sit in apparent oblivion.

Is it the blood on our plates, or the blood on the screen that we're avoiding?

Could be any number of reasons why our species needs the visual sound effects of suffering in the world whether it is on the news, or in the likes of classics such as *Apocalypse Now*—I enjoyed the film six times so far, with popcorn, and will again.

It might be soothing for our digestive tracts to feel: better them than us; a kind of comfort food as placating as restaurant music with sharp notes tossed in to stimulate our taste buds gone numb.

As cathartic as a diuretic purging us of our guilt attached to every juicy morsel we enjoy at someone else's—human or non-human—expense.

It is definitely easier to digest our fears and rage in the world around us, instead of inside our own little worlds.

Maybe that elk was onto something human.

~

When hunting for a meal
we stay on a random course
for tidbits here and there
to feed our bellies
        and our hearts.

—Mule Deer

11

Onto the Brilliance of Deer

In Montana, I spent a lot of time walking in the footprints of mule deer and whitetails, too lazy to make my own in the deep snow, too stubborn to follow in my own species' steps.

Native Americans honor deer as having a unique medicine for those of us who need to move past our human tendency to stay stuck in the mud of outworn beliefs and patterns of behavior.

When out in the snowy woods just before nightfall, I often met up with the same family of three mule deer. In polite deer fashion, we would stop at a safe distance of about fifteen yards from one another, look into each other's eyes for a brief moment, pay our silent respects, and continue on our way.

One evening, the male trotted fearlessly toward me and stopped by a cedar tree a few feet from where I stood in the snow.

With our eyes locked, he began snacking on one of the branches. After a few seconds that seemed an eternity, my eyes tired. I pulled my eyes away from the deer's gaze and moved on. I turned around. His eyes were still on me while he chewed his cedar salad.

They say people given deer medicine move from one place to the other, never staying in one place long enough to grow fat.

~

Your wings are behind your heart.
Open your heart and fly.

—Little Yellow Bird

12

Sometimes You Just Know

About eight years ago, I sent an email to Heart Math Institute asking what the heart frequency is of a pig, or any mammal compared to that of a human heart.

Their reply implied that my question was a stupid one.

In the film, *An Inconvenient Truth*, Al Gore tells us about a six-grader who asked his teacher if the edges of the South American and African continents fit together like two pieces in a puzzle. The teacher shamed the sixth-grader for asking what she thought to be an absurd question. It was teacher who was the ignorant one, however.

The student knew on some level what science already knew to be true: the two continents were once one.

That said, several years after I received Heart Math's scoffing response to my question, Heart Math published research regarding their findings that a horse's heart resonates in frequency with the human heart.

Sometimes you just know things though you may not have the resources to prove they're true on a more than personal level. We know from our animal instinct.

Non-human animals are already proven to have the capacity to *just know*. Science discovered that dolphins, canines, and other animals tested have the capacity to just know for example, the location of cancer in humans. You know this.

Sometimes, we *smell* things without being consciously aware that we know.

***

"I will write only simple, beautiful things I know and understand" is a line still resonating in my heart from *Little Women*. On that note:

I know the effect the frequency of love has on matter, including matters of the heart.

I know that when scientist Dr. Masaru Emoto projected loving thoughts onto still water, the water shape-shifted into beautiful geometric patterns. I saw it happen. He also showed hateful thoughts making unpleasant and fractured shapes in the water. Similar discordant shapes could be made by the sound of chalk scraping over a blackboard or the sound of a car's brake pads wearing thin.

I know there are healers in China and Thailand who positively *intend* away tumors in their patients. I saw on ultrasound a tumor disappear in a woman's abdomen as several healers stood around her and chanted instructions to her body to heal.

I know that when I put my hand on a miniature pony's little chest, I felt so overwhelmed by his love frequency coursing through me that my lungs felt too small to breathe in the magnitude of his compassion.

No scientific findings are available yet, but I know like an animal that a dog's heart, a cat's heart, a pig's heart, a rat's heart, an elephant's heart, any mammal's heart—not only a horse's heart—resonates in frequency with the human heart.

Pig hearts, because of their similarity in size to

the human heart, are under consideration for future transplants into humans. Wouldn't you think that a pig's heart would also need to have the same resonance in frequency to our own heart if it is to keep a human body alive?

Wouldn't you think it actually does?

And if this is true—and I *know* it is—a resonance in frequency is what makes a heart-to-heart connection possible with most any animal, if not all.

The probability became real to me many times, and once with a red dog named Rosie.

***

I was asked to give Rosie a Reiki-Polarity treatment; sort of *laying on of hands* combined with acupressure. Rosie had knee surgery six weeks prior and was still limping and in pain.

As I approached her, she looked worried. I saw in her eyes she was afraid I would hurt her. She saw in my eyes I was afraid she would bite me.

Pushing fear aside, I lightly touched Rosie's chest with my right hand while touching my own *heart* with my left. A heart-to-heart flow of energy connected us in feeling safe together.

Try it with someone. It works.

Feeling secure in our connection, Rosie willingly

received love's high frequency healing to the core of her being. I know. I could physically feel her body tension along with her knee spasm relax into pure bliss; an exalted feeling in her body that I could feel reflected in my own.

She made a flat run the next morning, the first time in six months.

Open, loving, and resilient like an animal can be, that Rosie is.

~

I am hard and compressed holding onto God.
I am soft and pliable holding onto you.

—Solid Rock

13

All We Can Be as Animals

Yearning to be all we can be is more than human.

It's animal.

Look at your canine friends who, like any dog according to science, may not be as smart as a pig.

Yet, Science did in fact prove that the average dog has taken the trouble to learn the meaning of at least two hundred words.

Think about it: Dogs have an affinity to understand our verbal language, one of the many ways they strive to enrich their relationship with us. They are known experts on our emotional and body language as well.

Yet, when you think about it, one wavelength of sound emanating from them holds for us a thousand *words* we as a species, have not been interested to fathom. Until recently, we were not close to scratching the surface.

We're the only animals afraid of feeling deeply connected to not only our natural environment and other species, but to our own species as well.

Acknowledging a bond with anyone unlike us, for instance in the way one holds a knife and fork, is scary. Our natural yearning to explore all that appears unlike us, but ultimately *is* us, is denied.

Excessive amounts of food, over- and under-the-counter drugs, religion, sex, cyberspace—every numbing binge leads to the *mourning* after.

Suppressing our true desires wreaks havoc and discontent in our bodies, in our lives, and in our environment; squeezing our true animal essence through the cracks in split, unwholesome, and sometimes criminal ways.

Aside from most of us and other domesticated animals under the influence of fear, there are a few empowered animals still on the planet who can lead us to peace, health, and happiness simply by our watching them be who they are.

The simple act of observing an animal in its true power can, if we let it, inspire us to resurrect our own animal nature, untainted deep within the burial grounds of our minds and bodies.

Non-human animals are masters of appreciation for the cycles and mysteries of life. If we would for a moment allow ourselves to be their students, they would help us reclaim our own animal wisdom in being our best in life and death.

The death cycle needn't be a time of sorrow. It can be a time of ultimate connection, self-discovery, and bliss.

An old dog in Montana passed up his cushy spot in the kitchen each night to sleep in below zero weather outside in the snow. He could have opted for the cushion on the porch if the kitchen was too hot, or if he wanted to be alone.

Obviously, his choice to lie on the hard, frozen earth beneath a tree bonded him more with his maker than the 'doggie bed'.

A terminally-ill dog told his human friend that although he felt intense physical pain, dying was as much an adventure as being born had been for him.

Both dogs lived and died with dignity and self-respect.

***

Self-respect wasn't invented by *high-minded* us. It is

easily detected in an animal's vigor when refusing to obey us.

Sweetgrass demands that I treat her with respect. How do I know this? She tells me.

When we're out for a walk, I have her by the leash. I want to go right. She wants to continue straight. I tug on the leash. Her fifteen pounds don't budge. I tug again.

She stands her ground. Looks me straight in the eye. I get it. I say, "please." The leash softens, and Sweetgrass is by my side again.

I did not train Sweetgrass to agree when she hears, "please" from me. She learned it on her own through observation. She noted how people's body language, facial expressions and voices softened whenever I said the word.

All bite and no bark if I should attempt to clean her ears without first asking permission.

***

Humor. Animals have it and they know when and how to use it.

Sweetgrass, like any animal, has her own brand of humor. It shows up when we're out hiking with her off leash behind me, and I'm off in my head obsessing about something.

Lacking patience for fretting of any kind with so much nature for us to sink into, Sweetgrass' habit of yanking me out of my one-track mind comes into play: she stops in my tracks behind me and waits for me to turn around.

Forgetting her game, assuming she's tired, I backtrack to pick her up. I bend down.

I lower my arms.

She bolts out from under me in joyful abandon, runs full speed ahead, takes her signature leap high into the air, and floats suspended for a nanosecond like a rabbit.

I lighten up. My stress is left behind me in a cloud of dust as I chase Sweetgrass' lead through a forest suddenly enchanting.

***

Animals can lead us to enchantment if we would follow them for a change.

By their understanding our verbal language, or teaching us respect, or filling us with more joy than our lungs can sometimes breathe in, we give ourselves permission to feel connected to them, to our own animal essence, to the Beauty within.

When I quiet my mind and settle into my body with any animal—dog, pig, cow, cat, horse, an insect with no name, a human—in that one pure moment, I feel at one with them.

Instead of feeling isolated in the web of life, I feel safe in Beauty. Secure in knowing that all is as nature intends.

***

We are not the only ones who yearn to feel Beauty. Science knows of one or two animal species who will spend days searching for opiates in the wild to help them remember.

Sweetgrass has not been known to search for opiates, but I do know she has an affinity for Beauty when 'losing' herself under the spell of natural light, reminiscent of our losing ourselves in a Monet. I always make sure the place we live in has enough sunlight to keep her spirit bright.

During one of our stays in Montana, our place did face south, but cedar trees claimed their stately presence in front of our windows; a shadow I feared would darken Sweetgrass' sunny disposition those six months of winter.

It happened that on the dreariest of days, Sweetgrass' passion for Beauty burned so strong, she found it wherever she was. The darkest corner included. Her tail wagged throughout that entire winter like it was linked to the Duracell bunny.

Her commitment to experience Beauty on a regular basis is the quality I aspire to most in being all we can be as animals.

~

… Enough

Even fleas chase after my sweet journey.

—Hummingbird

14

Romancing My Animal Self

I used to think loving my body meant standing naked before a mirror, staring at my thighs, and declaring, "I love you, thighs." Cellulite gives free radicals a life, they must be all right.

I used to think forcing my body into a shape I deemed fit was another way to accept it. Caring for my body meant subjecting it to a dictum of affirmations: declaring decrees as to what it would do for the state of my welfare, ordering it to look beautiful for me, telling it how it should make me feel.

I treated my body with the lack of respect people show in beating animals more intelligent than they. I saw my body not as a bright animal, but as a mindless lowlife bent on keeping me within the confines of its sleazy domain, sentenced by the Church to a life of shame.

Not anymore.

My religious crusade against my body ended on February 21, a long, long time ago when Time as I knew it was still a reckless teen.

It was night. My ten-day purification dietary fast by fire—the main element in brown rice according to Ayurvedic scriptures—was finally over.

I was out pacing the streets of Manhattan, obsessing about my creative block on the paper I had to write describing my rice fast experience, an assignment for a nutrition class I was in.

My intention had been to leave my East 74th Street apartment, walk fourteen blocks down Madison Avenue, gratify myself with the organic, low-fat vegan cookie I would buy, consume, and then quickly return home to write.

I walked the fourteen blocks to the cookie, savored it, swallowed it, turned around, and headed home; this time by way of snack-laden Lexington Avenue.

Once on Lexington, I mumbled, "what the hell", and *fell* into vanilla mounds of Ben & Jerry's (fewer calories than praline cream), two slices of plain pizza, a large-sized healthy popcorn (must be healthy, it was soaked in real butter), one *real* fruit jelly donut, and last but not least, two *protein* custard-cream donuts.

Finally, I managed the strength to pull myself off my path of destruction and headed back on Madison, home.

My two steady companions—guilt and self-disgust—were not with me on that trip. I had in fact walked the fourteen blocks and eaten the vegan cookie as planned, the reason for their absence. I had kept my commitment.

It wasn't my fault that my cravings were a reaction to being fed nothing but rice and water for ten days. Nor did I think I had anything to do with the sorry state of health my body subjected me to with its flip-flopping from hypo to hyperglycemia, dangerously poor digestion, and a weak immune system.

A few blocks later, my pancreas got the shakes; I could feel it trembling inside me just as I was coming out of Zabar's with remnants of chocolate éclair oozing out of the corners of my mouth. I broke into a cold sweat. I was in real trouble this time.

Moments later I was home, breathing deeply, very deeply—only my breath could save me. One panicky thought in that moment had the power to kill me, I believed. I swore to god that if I lived through this blunder, I would never again abuse my body.

Then, out of the sleaze, a soothing feeling washed over me, lending a translucent blue-green color to my mind's eye—what this world considers a sugar rush was in that moment a sacred, other worldly feeling. It was no less than a slam-dunk of a revelation:

My pancreas tried so hard to function under the intense workloads dumped on it during my food binges. Every organ in my body was constantly put under extreme duress by me.

As I thought about the thankless struggles of my loyal organs—my little victims—I felt remorse for the agonizing torture I inflicted on them.

I blamed them for my pain without once acknowledging them as the sacred, aware beings they are in truth:

Little animals with a consciousness of their own, a well-organized pack working to fulfill their life's purpose in keeping the alpha animal, my body, safe from harm and in optimum health.

Before my epiphany that night, my body was my property, the one domestic animal I neglected, and debased as I pleased.

My vital organs meant no more to me than

mere annoyances I had to bear.

That auspicious night a long time ago, I observed my body as an accurate reflection of who I was at the time.

Not in my mirror, but as my mirror.

My organs as clearly as if they were on exhibition in front of me, added up to the sum total of who I was.

They couldn't function under creative tension any better than I could in trying to deal with my assignment that night. They were unfocused, ungrounded, and as out of control as my mind.

When I think of the torment my body went through all those years, I want to run to the confession booth and dump my guilt on whoever is sitting there in the dark behind the polyester veil.

No wonder my organs were whacked out. I listened to their groans for the sole purpose of dictating the appropriate commands to make them obey me. "You are healthy, radiant, and full of vitality," as if milk and cheese came from happy cows.

If I considered my body regarding foods I wanted to gorge on, it was to make sure my fun would not be spoiled.

What an assault to my body's intelligence—to any animal's intelligence.

That night, my body and I began our journey of self-recovery; a venturing through dark regions to weed out *normal* human beliefs that warped our life all those years.

The more I faced those fears from a compassionate perspective toward humanity, the more I felt at home in my body.

Today, my body and I are no longer at each other's throats.

I put an end to blaming it for my mind-created misery. How could I continue to abuse someone with whom I had fallen so deeply in love?

My body got healthy from feeding on my new awareness. If I felt I was blocking its flow of energy in some way, I took care of the problem with the simplest of natural remedies: deep breathing the way animals do every moment of their lives.

Until my pancreas functioned well on its own, I would reassure it, "It's okay to have a little sweet. No need to rush. Easy on the insulin. You have plenty of time." My breath supplemented my words to *show* my pancreas it was not alone. I could feel it was impressed with my new non-violent way of communicating.

My immune system also began to hold less fear obvious in the fact that I haven't been sick in years.

I helped support and strengthen it by suggesting that instead of acting like a vicious attack dog whenever we had 'uninvited guests', it could loosen its grip for a change and let destructive intruders self-destruct without provoking them into matching our fear and aggression with more fighting and exhaustion for us.

Our non-reactive, more responsive attitude created an environment that was unsuitable for their conquer and destroy type of colonization.

***

I don't talk to my body anymore. Years have passed since this was necessary.

The need was lost when my body and I merged healthy and whole together as one.

As if we were ever separate.

As if I was ever not an animal.

~

What are you looking at?
I am looking at you looking at me.
What do you see?
Infinity.

—Communing with a fish

15

The Beached Flounder

I look into his eyes and feel pity knowing his pain will soon be on my plate.

Yet I see the sorrow in his eyes is for me, for what he sees: how I will waste his life floundering around in my own.

I watch him flip-flopping in the sand from left to right, right to left, gills flicking iridescent light—expanding and contracting on his search for meaning—scaling the sands of Time.

Finally, giving in to both sides, the beached flounder leaves all restriction behind, and me with a full plate.

Realizing he was more beautiful than I could be makes me wish the tables were turned for you and me.

Where Beauty need not sacrifice her flesh to help us see: in gratitude, instead of greed, like other animals is how we might be.

~

I am a passing cloud darkening your night for now.

—Dark Cloud

16

Blood Thirst

"I want to rip open your ribs and lick the blood between your lungs so I may taste who I am," words I splattered on paper a decade ago, and in a frenzy, dumped on the doorstep of my innocent, unsuspecting neighbor, Chris.

Not since that steamy August day has my primal truth surfaced from that deep a place within my being with such sudden, intense purity of purpose.

But my behavior is understandable in view of the fact that *carnivore* bleeds through our genes.

***

Have you wondered why Christ would suggest

that his followers eat his body and drink his blood? How can the embrace of cannibalism not be inherent in his choice of metaphor?

Did he choose the metaphor as a savvy marketing expert who knew we would accept it as relevant to our history of humans eating the flesh of other animals, and on occasion, our own species to gain sustenance for our souls as well as our bodies?

When we make love are we not after a piece of ourselves in our lover? Is a marriage not considered consummated (as in *consume-mate*?) until the event of sexual intercourse—the course closest to the dessert of actually ingesting one another?

Have you ever felt smothered to death by someone trying to *devour* you?

Ever salivated at the sight of someone you *love to death*, or *must* have?

***

In the case of Jeffrey Dahmer, wasn't he ravenous for his lost youth reflected in young boys? Didn't he say he ate them to assuage his guilt for wanting to possess their energy through sex?

For him, dining on his *lovers* was more Christian, less perverse than god forbid, having sex with them.

What would we do without cannibals such as Jeffrey Dahmer to remind us of what we are in the historic black holes of our hearts?

What are our *empty stomachs* craving when we drool at the mere thought of sinking our teeth into the flesh of an animal? Vitamin B12?

The taste of who we were or are yet to become?

We already know meat is the number one cause of colon cancer, heart disease, and a lot of other deadly diseases, including obesity. What are we after?

How is Jeffrey Dahmer's palate any different than ours, aside from the fact that he ate the flesh of human animals? Aren't we also cannibals lusting after the blood of animals who, in the larger scheme of life are our blood relatives?

***

Remember Hannibal Lektor in the film, *Silence of the Lambs*—the scene where he is in prison chewing on the flesh of his gate keeper? In the midst of his feast, a succulent leg of lamb lays abandoned on a plate by his side.

Is the author's message that feeding on a human is no different than partaking of a real *Lamb of God*?

Is his character a mockery of our own cannibalism? Our human *in*-humanity?

***

If you were to compare the miserable, degraded
life of our enslaved animals to that one day of
crucifixion in the life of Christ with women weep-
ing at his feet, wouldn't you think Christ never
had it as bad as the animals who suffer every day
of their lives; beat-up and sacrificed for the sake
of our insatiable blood thirst?

I wonder: are we not all little Hannibal Lek-
tors drunk on the flesh of animals who screamed
as loud for mercy as his victims?

If we are all connected in the web of life, and
if what happens in one corner of the cosmic
trampoline reverberates through all of us, then
isn't it also true that whatever horror is inflicted
on one of us, we all suffer it, consciously or not?

The river of pain rising with the blood
screams of billions of animals skinned, cut up, or
boiled alive each year—tortured heinously their
entire lives—most in factory farms that defile the
waters, the earth, the sky—we all ride the same
waves crashing through our core.

Hannibal Lecktor showed us a piece of ourselves, as did Dahmer, as did Christ. Will there come a time when we will demonstrate reverence for not only Christ, but for all of life?

Can we, with a huge amount of Beauty, accept our blood thirst in gratitude as an ancient rite of passage through our evolving predator nature, and then finally—will we move on?

If Christ was a vegetarian (there is strong evidence he was—read for starters the book by Keith Akers, *The Lost Religion of Jesus*) wouldn't it make perfect sense why he chose bread to represent his body, instead of a chunk of lamb served at Passover when the Last Supper took place?

Wouldn't it serve us to quickly get off our bloody laurels as the dominant beast and begin to do what Christ, Buddha, and other divinely famous animals have done?

Since compassion is an essential part of being an animal, isn't it time we switched from oppressors to leaders of the animal pack? Isn't it time we moved on to honoring all life, Mother Earth's included?

Before Life its self loses our bloodline.

~

Why obsessed with the mirror?
  I am so sad. I am so alone. I have no nest
  to call my own.
You don't look sad.
  Neither do you.

—Magpie

17

I Close My Eyes

For consolation, when the pain of thinking about our degradation of innocent animals consumes me to the point that I cannot breathe, I close my eyes and think of Kafka's *Penal Colony*.

In Kafka's story, a man is sentenced to death by pendulum. He is stretched spread-eagle on a rack. Each time the pendulum skims his body, its sharp blade scrapes off a layer of his *belongings;* first his clothes, then his epidermis, then dermis, then soft tissue.

With each swing of the pendulum, the man writhes—screams and bellows like someone whose sable coat is ripped off of his/her back might sound.

It is when Kafka's subject is trimmed down to the bare bones at the point of death, does he surrender to his fate, and in that moment—a surrender so tender—his eyes glow in bliss and peace.

He is redeemed. He has experienced Beauty.

I need to think that Beauty happens to all animals at the final moment they are strung up for slaughter; a sorry lie I tell myself to pretend that the consequences of our blood thirst are not all in vain, pun intended.

A few holocaust victims, human or non-human might have experienced Beauty at the point of death.

But no matter how you slice it, there's an ocean of dried blood on our hands.

~

If you go where the breezes blow way up high,
we will show your ego how to die.
Don't forget: Life is all about Death.
That is where we met;
on the slopes of no regret.

—Falcon Spirit

18

The Space Between

She scares me, this woman standing before me, looking through me as though I wasn't here. I am attracted and repulsed.

Tourists would see beauty in her face, smiling without secrecy, exposing her toothless mouth. My harsh imaginings tell me she lost her teeth gnawing at the bones of chickens whose plucked flesh seems to mask her face, plumping flabby folds around her mouth and jaw.

Yes, she looks colorful and pleasant enough— like the old peasant women you expect to see stalking these torrid Greek islands, their heads and shoulders cloaked in heavy black shawls.

But looking into this one's eyes, the whites having retreated long ago behind curtains of skin, I feel myself smack up against cold, black stone.

Her gaze so empty, I will die if she does not notice me.

Breaking into her deadpan glare, I enter the tar-swept density of her eyes. Suddenly, I see my mother's eyes stare back at me from her coma, looking through me—like a wolf who once was so focused on Sweetgrass behind me, he didn't see I was there to the point I felt I might not be.

What are you looking at? Answer me.

Small and stupid in the face of death, I turn away defeated and head down the scalding white beach.

***

I want dying to become second nature to me as it is for an animal.

When I was in advertising I had to write a line for a sheer polka-dotted shirt. I remember being intrigued by the transparent nothingness between the dots; the sheer implication of the connective tissue that holds together the proverbial web of life:

The invisible, omnipresent, silent death called *god* in most religions; experienced as peace, stillness, timelessness—the silence between the heartbeat—the nada between and within all things...an animal's natural habitat.

It is that elusive, yet omnipresent death we savor most when out in nature.

Whether I am feeling wonderment from fixing my naked eye on an itty-bitty patch of clover and experiencing the friendly magic gazing back at me; or accidentally brushing my elbow against poison oak and feeling surprised by its benign kiss in return; or drifting through the many shades of brown in Sweetgrass' eyes and seeing beyond the windows of my soul—I lose all sense of time.

Basking in the stillness of death is where all of nature seems to thrive. Where I feel most like an animal.

***

I wonder about my mother in her coma, the old toothless woman in Greece, and a person with Alzheimer's—are they all wafting in the space between?

I recall the times I floated mindlessly back to earth with a parachute, or back to my body without one, and I think maybe this is what they feel:

Life suspended in death.

When I ignore my thoughts to the point they no longer seem to exist, I am in those rare moments, a mindless animal tumbling ever so softly through emptiness; as intimate with death as I am so far willing to get.

***

Again, I stretch my mind around that see-through shirt and think: what if there were no polka-dots, but only the peeka-boo space between—a bare-skinned landscape, a blank sign diffusing all geographic synapses? I am struck *dead* by the thought of no thought, of seeing nothing.

Then—out of the nothingness—the shimmering, velvet reality of a black bear appears, an elusive animal running through the cedars on Candy Rock Mountain where I've been sitting all this time comes into focus, and I know I am home, again.

Not at my destination, but back on my journey to it in the space between.

~

When you cut down a tree, or step on an anthill, or pick a flower, you deny us our wonder.

—Desert Flower

19

Dandelions

They drifted in from out of nowhere. All three a holy trinity.

Their round, ethereal bodies hover together in the sweaty, gray air over Hoboken where I sit; a fool on the hill, smacking mosquitoes on my face.

My bare legs, their hot open pores inhaling pesticides from pale, stubby grass, itch for me to stop worrying about Lyme ticks.

Rather than get up and move, or stay and accept frustration, I keep my eye on the odd threesome before me.

Each whimsically is bouncing on air; inseparable yet, separate, equally distanced from the other

—maintaining about an inch of space between them.

Their fluffy, white bodies are in perfect symmetry at opposite ends of their upside-down triangle—pointedly free-falling to earth in a dreamy, slow motion descent.

These dandy, courageous little *lions* are taking their topsy-turvy world ever so light-heartedly, without hesitation, never stopping to figure out the magic that brought them together.

Suddenly, another mosquito I slap on my face bites the dust, and puff—the holy trinity is gone beyond a curve of space, swallowed up forever in the dense Hoboken sky.

Gone. Just as I was thinking about getting up to touch them, to forever hold them in my grasp. As if anyone could ever really hold on.

As if any animal other than human, would ever go against nature.

~

Why don't I itch after touching you?
  No need to get under your skin when you
  hold me in your heart as you do.
Thank you for your caress.
  Thank you for your finesse.

—Poison Oak

20

Throw out the Bears and Lions

It was the week before Christmas 2006, in Montana.

I told several people at lunch that I was looking forward to spending Christmas day hiking alone in Glacier Park.

After a few seconds of silence which felt like pity, I was asked if my dachshund, Sweetgrass, would be going with me.

No. Dogs are not allowed in Glacier Park. Besides, Sweetgrass, true to her breed, doesn't appreciate the cold.

The woman on my left told me I need to get myself a real dog, a Montana dog. She meant well.

The one sitting in front of me agreed. They felt sad for me. I began thinking I should feel sad, too.

What is bad about wanting the simplicity of Christmas in one of the few sanctified places left on earth—more holy than any church built by human hands? What is pathetic about yearning to enjoy goodwill toward all life—not just men—in the sparkling, stark silence found in nature, alone?

Like any animal, I sense a hallowed presence more in a dead tree in the Glacier burn area than in a glass of eggnog. Although I have seen a dog or two, find bliss in eggnog as I have.

***

I hear stories about people moving to Montana for love of the beauty and wildlife. Once they arrive, fear of nature gets under their skin, and they start itching to throw out the bears and lions.

I wonder if those new arrivals attend the same church of denial that prays for peace on earth without recognizing the obvious: the metaphorical lamb will never lie down with the lion if we keep pushing real lions along with the rest of wildlife off the planet.

Whether we are from California, Montana, or wherever, we hunger each year for more distractions, including more human offspring than we can care for, to fill us.

The irony is most of us may never get to indulge ourselves in the one luxury essential to our fulfillment: the realization that our underlying feelings of desolation are rooted in failure to appreciate the quickly disappearing natural world.

Bonding with nature is a sustainable way out of increasing loneliness. Fine art, music, literature: they fill us with the memory of what was, what could be.

Nature keeps us full with what *is*.

***

That Christmas my spirit was small. I had zilch compassion for my human counterparts. I felt shame and disgust for us all; for our narcissism at the sacrifice of the truly sacred.

I lost heart. I lost my connection to the Wild calling me home to holy communion to cleanse my spirit in the crystalline peace of Glacier Park. I lost my connection to the spirit of Christmas.

I lost my connection to humanity, to you.

How horrible if only humans remain on earth, breeding, breeding, breeding—billions more insatiable consumers spouting out of humanity's womb like worms gushing out of a rotting apple; our beautiful planet fermenting in our own demise.

We could soon meet the same fate as our pets.

If we don't take responsibility for the over-population dilemma, spay and neuter will eventually be mandated for humans. How could it not?

The Pope is diabolical. How can anyone go to impoverished areas and tell people as he recently has, to keep reproducing? The starving, church-fearing poor are brow-beaten into breeding what in reality, is more misery for them and for their living as well as unborn children.

***

When I look into a child's eyes, and sink into those watery pools, I drown in knowing that we are spoiling it not just for the bears and lions, but for all life.

We don't have to throw it all away.

A caregiver for children with special needs says these savants believe humans are at the lowest end of the evolutionary scale.

It makes perfect sense why one Dalai Lama chose to reincarnate as a Shih Tzu.

I would choose a dachshund.

Maybe a yellow jacket.

       —In the presence of a Shih Tzu, a savant of a different breed

21

Scapegoats

When someone is in a rage, s/he's acting like an animal, we assume.

In the past, when my temper came unleashed, I would call myself a *pig,* a *bitch* for acting out of control. Now, instead of calling myself names, I ask myself what is it I am so scared of that I have to attack everyone in my path; a more convenient response.

A non-human animal, who acts out rage *verbally* with a hiss or a growl, or physically with violence, is not acting like an animal anymore than I when consumed by fear and not feeling connected to my true animal essence.

Before racist name-calling became politically incorrect, white people would label black people as "lowlife animals." Like Whites, Blacks are animals, but *lowlife* is not an appropriate description for the majestic soul of any animal.

Recently, the human race began a journey of recognizing species-ism—a word that did not exist in the dictionary until the nineteen-seventies. A word that indicates a racist attitude toward species other than human.

Exploiting animals the way we once denigrated Blacks is a form—a species so to speak, of racism.

***

Imagine a new world where we stop debasing other animals because they remind us by their existence alone that they are our relatives.

A world where we no longer dump on Mother Earth as if we were acting out blame against our own mothers for making us a part of her.

A world where we no longer have dead animals on our dinner table to pretend we have the upper hand.

A world where we respect all life as made in the image of God, or more true to nature—in the image of Beauty.

A world where all one becomes all won.
Non-human animals don't need scapegoats.
We, however, think we do.

~

I am stillness in motion. Feel me.

—The Wind

22

Listening for a Change

Shamans believe wild animals are our allies, our power animals. Their presence—in the ethereal and, or physical world—helps us access our specific animal skills we might need at any given time on our journeys through life.

Shamans don't consider pets as power animals, except for rare exceptions.

I am not a shaman. I think of pets tame as they are, as power animals, except for rare exceptions. I use the shamanic phrase, *power animal,* as an inspiration to listen to our pets for a change.

Pets are magnificent wise souls reflecting to us our mystical animal essence. They can help us uncover and reclaim it, if we would listen.

Instead, most pets are condemned to spend their lives in boredom like wise elders confined in nursing homes.

When we aren't neglecting them, we're focusing on their cute looks, cornering them into souls they no longer recognize.

Relationships between us and our pets can be opportunities for growth, self-discovery and emotional evolution for all involved.

Sweetgrass, my power animal, is a dachshund bred to dig deep in hunting badgers underground. Her presence helps me lay the groundwork to venture past humanity's opinions on my search for hidden terrains of what is true for me, and possibly for you.

***

In Arizona, I encountered a power animal no bigger than the tip of my pinky. I never saw its kind before or again to this day. A silver insect shaped like a crescent moon on a rock close to where I sat. I had a sudden feeling someone was watching me. When I turned my head, it caught my eye.

Telepathically, this little insect told me I needed to slow down and take pauses in my life, the way a comma makes us take a breath between phrases.

Staring into the insect's eye, I was impressed by the immense energetic power of it.

Cautious about publicly confessing my having experienced intimacy with an insect, I did not share this encounter with anyone, fearful of looking stupid for identifying bugs as sympathetic. I needed substantial encouragement to face you with this one. It came to me a few years later.

On one of my drives back to California from Montana, I stopped by a used bookstore in Idaho.

Once inside the store, the first book to catch my eye was a tired, faded green hardcover published in the early nineteen-fifties: *Kinship with All Life*, by Allen Boone. I condescended to take it off the shelf thinking that my insights about animals transcended anything the author could possibly have written in this old book. Wrong.

Boone boldly admits in his book that he had an ongoing and sophisticated rapport with a house fly. What guts it must have taken for him to make this confession in the decade *before* the nineteen-sixties. But he did have a mighty power animal, the German Shepherd film star, Strongheart, prodding him along.

Thank you, Allen Boone and Strongheart.

***

Having an open mind and an open heart in listening to our animals—to what they have to give us besides affection, entertainment, and protection—not only supports them as power animals, but strengthens us in ways we may not imagine.

Science continues to discover that non-human animals have individual personalities—hopes and fears, talents, I.Q's, egos, depths of compassion, methods of fair play, problem-solving techniques, aspirations, abilities to meditate and reflect on changing their behavior patterns, knowledge of the future, how to experience bliss—not only within their own species, but within their own families.

The evidence is in:

We are not a superior species. We do not have a copyright on most admirable traits we call, human. We are animals, by any other name—as sweet, as sour.

When we listen for a change to non-human animals, we change.

When we listen to our own animal selves, we hear who we are, and the world changes.

When we become true to ourselves as animals, we listen not exclusively with our minds, or with our hearts, or with both. We listen with our whole bodies.

That could be enough.

Enough to lift all from the shadow of extinction.

~

When humanity wholly accepts
that we are all one,
dominion over the earth ceases to be,
and life as all one
becomes all won.

—Bald Eagle

When humanity wholly accepts
that we are all one,
dominion over the earth ceases to be,
and life as all one
becomes all won.

—Bald Eagle

Sweetgrass, what great vision of the Future do you hold personally for you?

I'm coming back as the Pope.

—Sweetgrass

Sweetgrass:

Teacher, Visionary, Manifestor

Don't believe for a moment that only we are creators of destiny, that only we can change the world. That only we have dreams for the future.

Sweetgrass has Vision like any animal. And like any non-human animal, she didn't have to read the book, *The Secret,* to know the Secret of manifesting dreams.

When inspired with a desire for something that feels deep in her gut, in her heart, in her mind, and in her body that it is her birthright to receive regardless of how mundane the object of her desire may seem, these are the steps she takes for foolproof manifestation:

1. Clarity. She is totally clear on what it is she wants.

2. Projecting. Without doubt or fear in her mind, heart, or energy, she sends her personal universe—me—a telepathic message; the same way she transmitted a message to me in my sleep the night there was a fire in her belly, Chapter 9.

3. Embracing. She holds in her mind's eye, and in her entire body, a vision of how the dream will look and feel once manifested.

4. Trusting. She doesn't stress. She knows that barking for her treat would make me tense and her manifesting delayed.

Instead, she relaxes like Buddha within close range to the source of her fulfillment—the cookie cabinet in this case—intending that the door will open, and that she is in the right place at the right time to behold her dream come true. She trusts that this is so, and so it is.

5. Intending. With her nose directed toward her prize, she holds her intent to receive without getting side-tracked by the intriguing odor wafting past the open window.

6. Self-Worth. She remembers with no doubt that she is worthy of receiving gifts the universe provides, but not too abundantly due to her size.

7. Patience. She perseveres in holding her intention. She knows the universe encompassing my room far across the galaxy of our tiny abode will fulfill her desire in *due* time.

8. Confidence. She trusts that I did receive her message. I finish what I am doing on the computer while feeling the urge to fulfill her wish. Though no evidence of manifestation is in sight, she knows it is already happening.

9. Determination. So close to attainment, nothing can distract her now. I enter the kitchen. She keeps her focus with no chance of losing it emotionally, without a blink. I open the cookie cabinet door above her.

10. Receiving. She opens her mouth wide and takes in spontaneous fulfillment. Utter joy ensues for having her treat manifested, and tasting better than she dreamed possible.

11. Gratitude. Sweetgrass knows this is her most important step as a master manifestor: as she savors her luscious dream come true, she lifts her head and darts a *thank you* straight from her heart through the universe into mine.

~

Following Sweetgrass' Lead

By following in Sweetgrass' step number '11', I first and foremost, thank Cathy Boggs, who, almost everyday for two years encouraged me to plow forward to the completion of this book. Thank you, Cathy, for not wavering in your belief in me. I am grateful for your friendship, editorial feedback, technical support, and both your and your husband Larry's patience.

I thank Promotions wizard, Jeff Marlow, CEO Scott Blum and Madisyn Taylor, and the entire staff at DailyOm.com for making my process of first advertising this book on their site a joyful experience for me. These people are evidence that not only is there hope for the future of humanity; we can actually take it to work with us.

I thank my longtime friend and work associate, Susan Clifton of Clifton.com for her excellent promotional design expertise and willingness to come through in short notice.

Thank you, Frank Critchlow, for your pragmatic advice and a space to write equipped with ocean breezes and green cuisine; delicious.

I thank Dominic, for his open-mind, support, and pride in me; Mary, for urging me to write; Palma, for her courage and honesty in questioning what I write; and Carol, for never questioning what I write and—for always showing confidence in me.

Liz and Bryan, thank you for cheering me on with your thumbs-up enthusiasm about this book.

Thank you, readers, for reading this book.

Last, and DEFINITELY NOT LEAST, I thank three GREAT muses (whose names I did not give to them) who inspired this book:

Bricabrac. The mare who nurtured, guided, and protected me as a child.

General. The incorrigible, gentle Dobeman who returned to me as Sweetgrass, my dachshund-sage, playmate, confidante, and jokester.

About the Author

Jane Broccolo is a spirit medium, animal communicator, energy therapist, Polarity Wellness Educator, Reiki Master, animal rights-welfare activist, freelance writer on human-animal connections, and founder of Talks With Pets and Animal Self Empowerment™ (ASE).

She has facilitated over a myriad of animals, human and non-human, in accessing and healing aspects of their animal selves.

Jane gives us new dimension and meaning to *animal communication*, extending it through every relationship in every area of our lives.

For scheduling workshops, teleseminars, interviews, speaking engagements, or private ASE phone sessions, please contact Jane at her website:

www.AnimalSelfEmpowerment.com